To: _____

From: _____

Date: _____

May God Bless You with an Angel

Lisa M. Bakos

Illustrations by Chris Shea

HARVEST HOUSE PUBLISHERS
EUGENE, OREGON

May God Bless You with an Angel

Text copyright © 2013 by Lisa M. Bakos

Artwork copyright © 2013 by Chris Shea,

Lifesighs Cards, PO Box 19446, San Diego, CA 92159

Published by Harvest House Publishers

Eugene, Oregon 97402

www.harvesthousepublishers.com

ISBN 978-0-7369-5397-9

Design and production by Mary pat Pino, Westport, Connecticut

All Scripture quotations are from the King James Version of the Bible.

Printed in China.

13 14 15 16 17 18 19 / LP / 10 9 8 7 6 5 4 3 2 1

I thank Christ Jesus our Lord who hath enabled me, for that he counted me faithful, putting me into the ministry.

1 Timothy 1:12

Dedicated to Steve, Alec, Jillian, and Josef, who continue to love me through it; to Julie, my fellow author and faithful sister; and to the guardian angels who watch over us all.

—Lisa

Dedicated to the angels who have crossed my path. You know who you are.

—Chris

May God bless you with an angel

For he commanded and they were created.

Psalm 148:5

to protect you with wide wings,

one to light and guard and guide you

This way···

Some have entertained angels unawares.

Hebrews 13:2

through the simplest of things.

When the bluebirds
sing each morning,

when you watch
your garden grow,

when you're giving
to all others,

and you reap all that you sow...

Let brotherly love continue.

Hebrews 13:1

when the crickets
serenade you,

when a freckle finds
your cheek,

when your dream is just too frightful,

Fear not.

Luke 1:13

or you're gentle to the meek...

Become as little children.

Matthew 18:3

when you catch a falling snowflake,

when the wind takes
your balloon,

when you need to say you're sorry,

Lay up his words in thine heart.

Job 22:22

or you see a harvest moon...

when you give someone
forgiveness,

when you're on your
knees in prayer,

And forgive us.

Matthew 6:12

when your heart is ever hopeful,

I know
I can fly . . .

and you let go of despair...

I can do all things.

Philippians 4:13

when you're down and brokenhearted,

when you see a
shooting star,

His tender mercies
are over all his works.

Psalm 145:9

when your life's a roller coaster,

or you travel near or far...

God is with thee
withersoever thou goest.

Joshua 1:9

when you're blowing out the candles,

Thou wilt light my candle.

Psalm 18:28

when you need
a Valentine,

when you hear the sound of thunder,

or you see a rainbow shine...

I do set my bow in the cloud.

Genesis 9:13

when you worry you
can't do it,

Continue in prayer.

Colossians 4:2

when you try
something that's new,

The Lord is my helper.

Hebrews 13:6

when you're singing in the shower,

or you whisper, "I love you"...

God is love.

1 John 4:8

when you see a ghost
or goblin,

when you gather
to say grace,

Be content with such
things as ye have.

Hebrews 13:5

when you decorate for Christmas,

or you see an angel's face...

I bring you good tidings of great joy.

Luke 2:10

may God bless you
with an angel

to protect you
with wide wings,

one to light and guard
and guide you

through the simplest
of things.

Only believe.

Mark 5:36